Nineteenth-Century
NEW YORK
in Rare Photographic Views

Edited by
Frederick S. Lightfoot

DOVER PUBLICATIONS, INC.
NEW YORK

CREDITS

The following views appear courtesy Mr. Benjamin Blom, City-
ana Gallery: 1, 2, 4, 5, 8–14, 16, 20–25, 29, 30, 32–43, 45–47,
50–54, 56, 58–61, 63, 64, 66, 67, 69–71, 73–76, 78, 80, 83, 84,
86, 90, 96, 98–102, 108, 110–112, 114, 117, 119, 125–127, 132,
146, 147.

All other views are from the Lightfoot Collection.

Copyright © 1981 by Frederick S. Lightfoot.
All rights reserved under Pan American and International Copyright Conventions.

Published in Canada by General Publishing Company, Ltd., 30
Lesmill Road, Don Mills, Toronto, Ontario.
Published in the United Kingdom by Constable and Company,
Ltd., 10 Orange Street, London WC2H 7EG.

Nineteenth-Century New York in Rare Photographic Views is a
new work, first published by Dover Publications, Inc., in 1981.

International Standard Book Number: 0-486-24137-8
Library of Congress Catalog Card Number: 80-71005

Manufactured in the United States of America
Dover Publications, Inc.
180 Varick Street
New York, N.Y. 10014

INTRODUCTION

THE STEREOGRAPH

It is only fairly recently that many photohistorians have begun to appreciate the tremendous importance of the stereograph, the double-image photograph which mysteriously yields a three-dimensional scene when viewed through a stereoscope. The stereograph was far and away the main medium for outdoor photography from the 1850s on, as literally millions of stereoscopic negatives were produced for the manufacture of images to be sold to the general public. Their subject matter included virtually every aspect of the natural world and the culture and life of man then accessible to the camera.

For the traveler seeking pictorial souvenirs of places visited, the stereograph anticipated the postcard. For the Victorian parlor, the basket of stereographs on a side table, replenished from time to time, was a predecessor of television. Hotels, dentists' offices and other public places had stereographs on hand, sometimes mounted on a rotating belt inside a cabinet viewer, for the diversion of their patrons. The equivalent of a penny arcade was created by one entrepreneur who assembled a large number of cabinet viewers filled with stereographs, and transported them from town to town.

Photographers in thousands of cities, towns and villages published substantial series of views of their locales. Large cities often had several galleries that specialized in the photographing and publishing of the pictures, and there were wholesale distributors who enabled them to sell their products nationwide and even abroad.

The amusement aspect of the stereograph, which reminded contemporary critics of various optical toys that had been popular previously, tended to limit serious consideration of its artistic merits, and this undoubtedly has influenced photohistorians to underrate it. Yet, from its earliest beginnings, the stereograph was recognized as a medium worthy of respect by some of the men who went out on city streets and to the countryside with their stereoscopic cameras, and by some people who built serious collections of stereographs. Oliver Wendell Holmes, in particular, prepared enthusiastic articles on them for the *Atlantic Monthly* in 1859 and 1861, and also invented a simpler stereoscope that could be produced very cheaply. Both his articles and his viewer persuaded many cultured readers to start substantial collections of stereographs for their private libraries.

Incidentally, the pursuit of improved lenses, shutters, and materials for negatives and prints that would make finer stereographs possible led to major technical advances for photography as a whole.

So great was the craze for stereographs that, according to a well-researched analysis by William C. Darrah, some 12,000 photographers in the United States and Canada alone turned out over five million different stereographs, a high percent of them of at least acceptable quality for historical reference.

The sales of stereographs waxed and waned at intervals for about 70 years in the United States, after which many families relegated their accumulation of them to the attic or the trash bin. Fortunately, significant quantities survived, and a small number of perceptive collectors, both private individuals and museum curators, salvaged them whenever they became available. Today, their collections constitute an incomparable treasure trove of authentic images of the nineteenth century.

NEW YORK IN STEREOGRAPHS

In the present volume, one of a series that Dover Publications has devoted to images of old New York, it is the streets and buildings of the city, as recorded in stereographs, that are featured. Only one half of each stereograph is reproduced.

As will quickly be evident from the attributions of the pictures, we are heavily indebted to the firm of the Anthony brothers, Edward and Henry, for the most superb images. In 1859, Henry Anthony became the first experimenter in the United States to perfect instantaneous photographs; the instantaneous views of Broadway and other streets published by the Anthonys won immediate international acclaim. The photographic artists who worked for the Anthony firm were sent out to record both sides of many blocks and stretches of Broadway, as well as of a few streets that branched off it. Certain blocks were taken repeatedly over a period of about 12 years. Towards the end of this time, the more convenient dry plate was often employed. Since it had a slower emulsion than the old wet plate, the feature of stopping motion was sacrificed. However, in 1880 the Anthonys brought out a new emulsion for dry plates which was much faster, and they commissioned a series of instantaneous stereographs to demonstrate its properties.

With some exceptions, we are not able to identify the publishers of many stereographs of New York other than those of the Anthonys. For reasons unknown, most publishers failed to have their names printed on the cardboard mounts of their stereographs, and simply gave them titles such as "American Views." It is possible that the intensive research now under way in this field will clear up some of the mysteries of the sources of the views, and perhaps even the names of the photographers who made the negatives.

To a limited extent, halves of stereographs were trimmed and mounted on carte-de-visite blanks. In the 1870s to the 1890s, there were also some photographs sold on "cabinet" cards, roughly four by six inches, for persons who did not enjoy stereographs. In the present volume, Plates 88, 136 and 141 are derived from such cards.

THE BACKGROUND OF THE VIEWS

New York in the 1860s and 1870s possessed a combination of charm and relatively unsophisticated flamboyance that it was destined to lose by the turn of the century.

Few buildings were over five stories high — about all that most people could be expected to climb, as passenger elevators were unknown until 1859 and were a novelty for some years thereafter. Church spires still reached higher than the towers of Mammon. Thus there was a certain degree of intimacy in the relation be-

tween man and building which was strengthened by abundant signs that told whose stores or offices were within the buildings. Because shops and stores were mostly small, owners as well as salespeople came in frequent touch with customers. In summer, shopkeepers often had awnings over the sidewalks in front of their shops to spare windowshoppers the heat of the sun.

A walk on Broadway, which was the business and cultural spine of the city, could be a delight, and countless writers, artists and photographers applied their talents in trying to capture its remarkable vitality. More or less typical of many descriptions in magazines and guidebooks are the following excerpts from *New York Illustrated* (1883) and an article from *Harper's Monthly:*

> It is not only a channel of commercial traffic, but a favorite promenade of the idler and pleasure-seeker, and though the acquaintances of a man be few, a walk up or down Broadway is sure to confront him with someone that he knows.
>
> The crowd is not distinctly fashionable, though well-dressed people predominate; workmen in fustian and poverty-stricken work-girls appear in the procession, besides threadbare adventurers and the abject devotees of the gutter. It is a crowd greater in numbers and steadier in its flow than anything London can show in Fleet Street or the Strand, and it mixes up the most dissimilar elements of nationality and condition. The night is never so dark or so stormy that the footfall of pedestrians and the rumbling of vehicles are altogether hushed. The occupants of the front-rooms of the hotels, waking at any hour, can still hear the reverberations of the traffic, which swell toward morning into a deafening roar, and continue without lull throughout the day. The stream is endless. When all the rest of the city is asleep, Broadway is awake, and looking through its vista between the two bead-like strings of lamps, we still see some pedestrians plodding along on various missions of crime, industry, pleasure or charity.
>
> It has a Champagne sparkle even in the parts where business is supreme; its tread is elastic, buoyant, and almost rhythmic, as it follows the rattle and roar of the vehicles; and that rattle and roar, made by the pressure of hundreds of wheels and hoofs on a resonant pavement, are like the *crescendo* movement

of a heroic symphony. Nervous people and people from the country cannot enjoy it; it is bewildering, painfully so, to them; but the active citizen whose nerves are in good condition finds stimulation in the friction and the noise.

The variety of architecture is extraordinary. Every material has been used in every style—brick, iron, glass, marble, granite, brown stone, yellow stone, wood and stucco. Small, modest dwellings of a much earlier period, with old-fashioned dormer-windows projecting from the upper story, and modern plate-glass windows inserted in the lower story, are threatened with suffocation by buildings twice or three times their height.

The Sierras are not more serrated than the cornice lines of Broadway, and the effect is not at all unsatisfactory to an artistic eye. Sign-boards hang out and the flag-staffs rise from nearly every building. On a gala day, when all the patriotic bunting is unfolded, the view is more brilliant and ragged than ever; but what engages us most is the crowd—that uneasy mass of black dots which resemble the pen-and-ink kisses of an amorous correspondent.

Bank messengers with actual bags of gold and packages of paper convertible into gold; office-boys with saucy faces and no less saucy manners; shrewd detectives with quiet, unobtrusive ways, altogether unsuspicious; telegraph boys in neat uniforms, carrying yellow envelopes that contain words penned ten minutes previously in California; railway magnates more important than many kings; spruce clerks and laborious porters—are included in the throng which passes before us in an almost solid body.

All is not toil and trouble with the merchants, however. Across the way is the white marble facade of a celebrated restaurant, where, after a successful stroke of business, a lucky handling of wheat or Erie, the masters of the situation make merry over the costly vintages of Champagne and Burgundy, sometimes prolonging their revelry to an hour when all the adjacent streets are dark and vacant, and Trinity spire points solemnly to the deep blue night sky.

Soon after six o'clock the high pressure of the traffic down town abates, the offices are closed, a single lamp being left burning in each to reveal the interiors to the policeman, and the tired-out workers seek their homes. By nine o'clock the street is quiet. A few pedestrians pass to and from the Brooklyn ferries at White-hall. Between midnight and four o'clock the telegraph and newspaper offices send out their wearied operatives. The street is never quite empty, but the rapid change which takes place at night-fall, previous to which every stone and flag has seemed to have a voice, suggests a visitation of palsy.

A short distance north of Trinity, Park Row slants off from Broadway, being separated from the latter thoroughfare by the new Post-office and City Hall park. Lights are burning over there all night. Men smirched with ink and pale with toil are coming and going constantly. Those high buildings are the offices of the great morning newspapers—the *Herald*, the *Times*, the *Tribune*, the *Sun*, and the *World*. The upper stories, in which the editorial and composing rooms are situated, blaze with light, and on the ground-floor, a paler light shows the advertising rooms, where a few sleepy clerks await the last advertisements.

While the lower part of Broadway is filled during the day with urgent business men and is deserted at night, the upper part is chosen for purchases and promenade by a much more brilliant throng, and is busy both day and night.

About two miles from the foot of the street the northward-bound traveller finds himself emerging from the close quarters of the street into one of those verdurous squares which lend a great charm to the city. In the mornings and afternoons the benches and asphalt walks of this bit of country in town are crowded with white-capped nurse-maids attending prettily dressed children; more or less disagreeable idlers, varying in distinction from the tramp to the slightly overcome tippler; and the pedestrians, who are glad enough to vary the monotony of the flag-stone sidewalk with a glimpse of the smooth grass-plats and the shelter of the trees. In the evenings lovers in pairs take the place of the *bonnes*, and the club man does not wholly despise the opportunity for meditation afforded by the benches, which are inclosed by grass and foliage, and near the tranquilizing murmur of the fountain. The lamps hang among the foliage, and the square is bounded by high buildings; the bells of the horse-cars and the rattle of other vehicles are half subdued, and the trees give one a sense of sequestration, although a few strides would take us back on the street again.

Looking out from Union Square, as this oasis in the desert of buildings is called, we get an idea of how interminable a Broadway crowd is.

About a quarter of a mile farther north Madison Square relieves the confinement of the street with fountains, grass, shrubs, and trees, and between the two such a parade may be seen on a fine afternoon, especially Saturdays, as no other city in America, and few other cities in the world, can show. The great retail houses of the Stewarts, the Tiffanys, the Arnolds and Constables, and the Lords and Taylors, are concentrated within these limits or in the immediate neighborhood, and woman in her most elegant attire appears in quest of new additions to her already voluminous apparel.

There was another major, but decidedly less glamorous shopping artery from Chatham Square on up The Bowery. Fifth Avenue, though, remained a prime residential area until many years later.

The commerce of Broadway overflowed into its side streets; beyond there came residential blocks for the rich and the poor. North of 14th Street, the well-to-do predominated, especially by the 1870s.

Until fairly late in the century, Manhattan north of 59th Street was quire rural. The sport of shooting snipe on the opposite Jersey shore might be a thing of the past, but there were rowboat stations for fishermen anxious to try for striped bass in the Harlem River or at Hell Gate, and large picnic grounds for less energetic recreation. Small farms, breweries, lumberyards and the like were dotted around the waterfront and interior, not yet forced out by rising land prices.

Transportation in the city was provided by numerous omnibus lines. Their horse-drawn vehicles followed routes north-south or crosstown, sometimes parallel to the horsecar railways that operated on many avenues and streets. Traffic jams and bad weather often made this surface travel agonizingly slow, so that "rapid transit" by elevated railroad became a necessity. The construction of elevated lines in the 1870s opened upper Manhattan to intensive development, while the completion of the Brooklyn Bridge in 1883 spurred heavier settlement in Brooklyn. In the process, older neighborhoods were abandoned by the middle class and often deteriorated.

Neither the stereograph nor any other form of photograph documented all the nearly explosive expansion of the city in the nineteenth century, partly because, as Mary Black has pointed out, it was characteristic of the times for publishers of photographs to concentrate on what the city could be proud of. Still, as the plates in this book demonstrate, they did give us a remarkably rich sampling of their world.

The views follow a geographic arrangement: the waterfront, lower Manhattan along Broadway to Union Square, north to Madison Square and the West Side, the East Side, "upper" Manhattan, the boroughs.

The assistance of James Spero, particularly in defining architectural details, and of the New-York Historical Society in determining the circumstances of Plate 44, is acknowledged with gratitude.

FREDERICK S. LIGHTFOOT

CONTENTS

1. **Reception of the Prince of Wales at the Battery, October 11, 1860; E. Anthony.** The year 1860 was one of exciting "firsts" for New York. The steamship *Great Eastern*, then the largest ship in the world, made its first trip to the port. Japanese ambassadors, on their first mission to the United States, also came to New York (see No. 15). And the Prince of Wales (later Edward VII) became the first heir to the British throne to include New York in a tour of America. Disembarking from the cutter *Harriet Lane* at the Battery, the Prince was greeted by Mayor Fernando Wood. There then followed a review of the troops (shown here, with the spire of Trinity Church in the background) and a gala parade up Broadway. The next evening the Prince was feted at the now-legendary ball given in his honor at the Academy of Music (see No. 71).

2. **Castle Garden, ca. 1866; E. & H. T. Anthony & Co.** In 1807 a fort, later named Castle Clinton, was built at the Battery to protect the harbor. Leased by the city in 1824, it was converted into an amusement spot named Castle Garden. It was transformed in 1845 into the concert hall where, in 1850, Jenny Lind made her spectacular American debut under the astute management of P. T. Barnum. In 1855, eleven years before this picture was taken, the structure became the city's reception center for the immigrants from foreign lands who disembarked at New York. As many as 10,000 a day received temporary shelter here, and were given help in contacting friends, relatives or reliable social agencies and boardinghouses. The continuous waves of immigration gave New York a polyglot population which contributed fresh vitality to the city's cultural and economic life. It was not until 1891 that the immigrant station was moved to Ellis Island. Castle Clinton was converted into an aquarium, delighting New Yorkers until the 1940s. It has now been restored to its original appearance.

3. The Barge Office at the Battery, ca. 1883; Continent Stereoscopic Company. This striking Romanesque Revival building at the Battery, made of granite, was primarily intended as the office for the Revenue Service. Construction began in 1880; the building opened on January 3, 1883. It was later the landing place for the government ferry to Ellis Island. In 1911 it was demolished.

4. Panorama of South Street from the Manhattan Pier of the Brooklyn Bridge, 1874; publisher unknown. The buildings (many of them of the Federal period) that lined South Street, shown here at James Slip (right), had originally been the countinghouses and stores and offices from which Manhattan merchants had conducted worldwide trade during the first half of the century. But by the end of the Civil War, South Street had lost its supremacy, steamships with international cargoes berthed at piers on the Hudson River and these buildings were being used as warehouses, a clothing store, a boarding-house, a liquor house, etc.

5. View on West Street, ca. 1880; publisher unknown. By the 1880s, after the great shift of shipping to the Hudson River, activity on West Street was intense. So many wagons were engaged in hauling produce, oysters (there were many oyster barges in the vicinity) and other merchandise that traffic frequently became completed snarled. The drivers seem resigned to a long wait.

904

6.   Omnibuses starting from South Ferry, 1861; E. Anthony. In 1831 omnibuses (also called stages), built by John Stephenson, were introduced as the principal means of public transportation in New York. Although they were generally replaced by the horse-drawn streetcar in the 1850s, they remained the sole means of public transport on Broadway south of 14th Street until 1885. As the omnibuses were small, it took a large number of them to accommodate the public. Writers frequently commented on their profusion (and attendant noise) as they rattled up and down Broadway. This view looks north up Whitehall Street. The large building is the Corn and Produce Exchange, built between Pearl and Water Streets in 1861.

7. **Omnibuses at South Ferry, ca. 1865; George W. Thorne.** Passengers entered an omnibus through a door at the rear. Climbing the high steps to the door was awkward for a lady in the era of the hoop skirt. The driver was fully exposed to the elements, and communicated with his passengers through an opening in the roof. Passengers on the stage signaled the driver to stop by pulling a leather strap attached to his leg.

8. **The east side of Broadway, looking south to Bowling Green, 1865; George W. Thorne.** The southernmost section of Broadway originally was lined with fine private residences and boarding-houses, some of which were converted to offices for consular agents, shipping companies, etc. By the 1860s, large new buildings had replaced many of the older ones, and they, in turn, would be torn down to make room for towering steel-frame structures by 1900. Some of the buildings in this view are draped in mourning for the Lincoln funeral procession of April 25. The cortège went up Broadway to the Hudson River depot, from which it continued its trip to Illinois.

9. **Looking up Broadway near Trinity Church, ca. 1871; E. & H. T. Anthony & Co.** Designed by Richard Upjohn and build of brown sandstone in 1846, Trinity Church occupies the site of previous churches, the earliest dating back to the seventeenth century. Its yard, enclosing the graves and tombs of William Bradford the printer, General Phil Kearney ("the bravest of the brave"), Albert Gallatin, Alexander Hamilton, Captain James Lawrence and Robert Fulton, among others, has long been both an historic shrine and a pleasant stopping place in the midst of the turmoil of Broadway. Trinity Parish was one of the largest property holders in nineteenth-century New York; much of its wealth came from rents collected from the slum tenements it owned.

10. Looking across the Hudson River from Trinity Spire, ca. 1868; E. & H. T. Anthony & Co. The steeple of Trinity Church, 284 feet high, afforded superb vistas in the 1860s when it stood higher than adjacent buildings and served as a reference point by which local directions were given. Nestled in the middle of this photograph, one of the few taken from the spire, are dormered Federal houses dating from the area's residential past.

11. **Looking up Broadway near Wall Street, 1865; E. & H. T. Anthony & Co.** This is an interesting picture, partly because, like No. 8, it shows buildings draped in mourning for the Lincoln funeral, and partly because it shows dramatically, by the contrasting buildings on either side of Wall Street, the transition from the older plain, dormered style of architecture to the imposing new Italianate style intended for banks, law offices and brokerage firms.

12. **Wall Street from the corner of Broad Street, ca. 1865; E. & H. T. Anthony & Co.** This instantaneous photograph is remarkable for its sharpness of detail extending all the way down the half mile of Wall Street to the masts of the ships docked on the East River. The classical building at the left, opened in 1824 as the New York branch of the Bank of the United States, became the United States Assay Office in 1853. It received deposits of gold and silver and paid for them in coin or stamped bars. When the building was demolished in 1915, its facade was salvaged and was reerected at the Metropolitan Museum in 1924, where it now graces the American Wing.

13.   **Looking east down Wall Street toward the old Merchants' Exchange, ca. 1870; publisher unknown.** The large multicolumned building down the street, designed by Isaiah Rogers and built in 1836 to replace the Merchants' Exchange destroyed in the great fire of 1835, was bought by the federal government in 1862 to serve as New York's Custom House. Constructed of Quincy granite, it was 200 feet long and 160 feet deep, 77 feet high and had a rotunda 80 feet high. Despite its size, critics described it as unsuited for its purpose because its interior was "dark, damp, inconvenient, badly ventilated." When a much larger Custom House was erected at the foot of Broadway in 1902–07, the new owners skillfully enlarged the old building by adding four stories.

14. **The New York Stock Exchange, Broad Street, ca. 1868; E. & H. T. Anthony & Co.** The New York Stock Exchange can trace its origin to 1792, when 24 brokers signed an agreement under a buttonwood tree on Wall Street. The white structure shown here was erected in 1865, and was subsequently much enlarged and altered. By 1868, the special materials and techniques required to produce instantaneous photographs were seldom employed by New York photographers. Thus the shifting figures clustered at the open-air curb market east of the Stock Exchange appear as "ghosts" in this picture.

15. Lower Broadway, north toward St. Paul's Chapel, 1860; George W. Thorne. In the 1850s Commodore Matthew C. Perry had "opened" Japan. In 1860 the Japanese sent an embassy to the United States, their first to any foreign nation. Broadway was decked with American and Japanese flags to greet the novel visitors when they arrived in the city from Philadelphia on June 16. Until the Japanese left for Japan on June 29, they were the center of attention. The highlight of their stay was a brilliant ball given at the Metropolitan Hotel on June 18.

16. The Western Union Telegraph Company Building, ca. 1875; publisher unknown. A block south of St. Paul's Chapel, on the corner of Dey Street, the Western Union Telegraph Co. erected, in 1872–75, what was a tremendous building for its time. Its height of 230 feet was made possible by the use of the passenger elevator, a recent development. The bold exterior of George B. Post's building—red pressed brick, granite and marble—made some observers hope that passing years might weather it to a gentler contrast. About 100 telegraph operators worked here. The building, open 24 hours a day, was brightly lighted at night. A ball atop the building, synchronized with the Naval Observatory in Washington, D.C., fell at noon, and was used by mariners in the harbor to set their chronometers.

17. The Loew Bridge, St. Paul's Chapel and the Astor House, 1867–68; London Stereoscopic Company. The heavy traffic on Broadway induced the city's Board of Aldermen to recommend "aerial bridges" across the street in 1852. Actual approval for one at Fulton Street, heartily urged by Genin the Hatter, was delayed until 1866. The Loew Bridge, as it was called, exceeded the approved price of $15,000 by $9,000. It cost another $9,900 to tear it down in 1868, after Knox the Hatter (Genin's archrival) claimed it obstructed light to his store and it was found to attract disreputable loiterers!

18. Broadway, north from Fulton Street, 1865; E. & H. T. Anthony & Co. The busiest intersection on Broadway was the junction with Park Row, where the terminus of several horsecar lines brought thousands of employees and customers to the financial and commercial businesses of the area. The Anthonys published many stereographs of the intersection, but this one has special interest for the bricks piled up at the right, all that remained of Barnum's Museum, a center of popular entertainment since 1841, which burned down July 13, 1865. The cupola of City Hall is visible in the distance.

19. **The bar and lunchroom of Nash & Fuller at 39, 40 and 41 Park Row, ca. 1870; Blauvelt & Co.** In the 1850s, much of the new business activity of the city was centered on Park Row, Chatham Square and The Bowery. The buildings on Park Row housed the offices of many newspapers and periodicals, as well as a number of restaurants, some of them in the basements. The garlands and festoons of greens in this view indicate that it was taken at Christmastime.

20. Park Row, south toward the Times Building, 1860; E. Anthony. Founded in 1851, the *New York Times* quickly became one of the foremost national papers. This Italianate structure was built in 1857–58 to house the entire operation from editorial offices to the presses, which were set up in the base- ment. At night, when most of downtown New York was quiet, this building was bustling, with clouds of steam pouring out of its smokestack and the side- walks shaking from the vibration of the presses. In 1889 the *Times* built a new structure, which still stands, on the same site.

21. **Park Row, south to the new Post Office (right), 1880; E. & H. T. Anthony & Co.** This view gives an excellent impression of the traffic around noon. In rush hours, the jam at Broadway sometimes was so severe that nothing moved for ten minutes, while a special squad of police ran around frantically trying to unsnarl it. In the distance is St. Paul's Chapel. The new Post Office, which also housed some federal courts and offices, was designed by A. B. Mullett and completed in 1875 at a cost of $6 million. Never adequate to its purpose and generally regarded as an eyesore, it was demolished in 1938–39. Its site is now part of City Hall Park.

22.   Park Row, north from Printing House Square, 1880; E. & H. T. Anthony & Co. Printing House Square took its name from the large number of newspapers that had offices in the immediate vicinity. In this view, at the extreme left, is the tall building that housed the *Staats-Zeitung*, a leading German-language newspaper. The edge of the Tribune Building (1875) is visible at the right, at the northern end of Nassau Street. At street level is the edge of the base of Ernst Plassmann's statue of Benjamin Franklin, honored as one of the nation's most famous printers. At this time, Nassau Street was noted for its antiquarian bookshops. In the distance, bridging Park Row, is a station of one of the elevated lines. Notable in this view are the utility poles, the one at the right having nine crossarms. As the telephone and other systems grew, the size of these poles became even more unwieldy, sometimes boasting as many as 25 crossarms. While city fathers decided that the lines had best go underground, little was done until the blizzard of 1888 toppled many of the poles.

23. Fourth of July, 1860 — troops enter City Hall Park from Tryon Row; E. Anthony. During 1859 and 1860, the Anthonys seemed to be trying to record all the major events in the city on their stereographs. One result was an excellent series of pictures of the 1860 celebration of the Fourth of July, a holiday then celebrated with considerably more patriotic fervor than it is today. This vantage point was chosen to capture the parade as it came to City Hall Park. At the left is the city's Hall of Records, where land records were stored. Built in 1757 as the Provost Prison, it stirred unhappy memories of the cruel treatment of American prisoners within its walls during the British occupation of the city in the Revolution. It was demolished in 1904. The Tryon Row Buildings were later torn down and the Staats-Zeitung Building (See No. 22) rose on the site.

24. **Fourth of July, 1860 — the cavalry; E. Anthony.** The dust raised by the horses partially obscures the Tryon Row Building.

25. Fourth of July, 1860 — the crowd disperses; E. Anthony. The series of pictures concluded with one of the spectators strolling from the scene. In a way, the Anthonys were anticipating, within a group of stills, the possibility of the motion picture.

26. **Billboards, 1866; E. & H. T. Anthony & Co.**
The City Hall Park area had billboards where the advertisements for theaters and other places of amusement were posted. It is again the Anthonys who had the imagination to record them on several occasions. Here are represented Barnum's Museum, which tried to stress its "moral plays," Niblo's Garden, the Olympic Theatre and the Union Course racetrack. The Ravels were famed for "marvelous pantomime" in "every strange costume from crowned king to skeleton death." The next attraction at Niblo's Garden was the historic presentation of *The Black Crook*.

27. **The Astor House, ca. 1874; E. & H. T. An-thony & Co.** Built on Broadway just north of St. Paul's Chapel, between Vesey and Barclay Streets, was the Astor House. Opened in 1836, for many years it fulfilled the intention of its builder, John Jacob Astor, of being the finest hotel in the country. Designed by Isaiah Rogers in the Greek Revival style, it had an interior garden and fountain, as well as a dining room noted for its cuisine and clientele. Decisions affecting six presidential campaigns and other major national events were made here by Thurlow Weed and other important politicians who resided in the hotel for various lengths of time. The venerable structure was demolished in 1926. In this view, the Western Union Building can be seen farther south on Broadway.

28. Broadway, north from Barnum's Museum, 1860; E. Anthony. P. T. Barnum allowed the Anthonys' men to photograph Broadway from the balcony of his museum, a privilege they took advantage of more than once. This picture is packed with interesting detail — the horsecar for Yorkville at the right, the varied designs of the omnibuses, different types of wagons and the pedestrians' costumes.

29. **Broadway, south from the corner of Murray Street to Barnum's American Museum, 1860; E. Anthony.** We are now looking in the opposite direction from that of No. 28. Barnum had purchased the building in 1841 from Scudder's Museum, for which the structure had been built in 1830. Enlarged in 1843 and 1850, the American Museum was not a museum as we conceive of it today; rather it was a melange of collections of curios, menagerie, freak shows, and presentations in the "Moral Lecture Room" (a neat circumlocution for "theater"). The banner fluttering from the museum is for the "What-Is-It," one of Barnum's freaks. The popular center of amusement came to a fiery end on July 13, 1865. Barnum reopened his Museum, but at another location. The vertical sign at the right — "Silks, Trimmings, etc." is a reminder that the textile center had not yet moved up Broadway.

30. Broadway, south from the corner of Chambers Street, ca. 1865. E. & H. T. Anthony & Co. This view, with City Hall Park on the left, was taken from the A. T. Stewart Store (see No. 34). The steeple to the left belongs to Trinity Church, that on the right to St. Paul's Chapel. Between the two the Astor House can be seen. Note the wagon at right angles to the curb and the crates piled up on the sidewalk. Obstructing traffic and pedestrians was a problem at least as far back as the 1860s.

31. Park Place from Broadway, ca. 1869; E. & H. T. Anthony & Co. A great many businesses were located on Broadway's side streets, where rents were cheaper. The bank fronts on Broadway, but the shops down the street advertise rattan furniture, fireworks, glass shades, printers and polishes, among other things.

32. **Broadway, north from City Hall Park, ca. 1870; E. & H. T. Anthony & Co.** This is one of the very few instantaneous photographs published by the Anthonys after 1868 and before the 1880 series. As the banner above Broadway shows, the blocks across from and directly above City Hall had become a focus for manufacturers of safes, firearms, and scales. The building at the end of the park is A. T. Stewart's Store.

33. City Hall from Broadway, 1865; E. & H. T. Anthony & Co. City Hall was one of the most frequently photographed buildings in New York, probably because it was (and still is) considered one of the most beautiful structures in the United States. Designed in a heavily French-influenced Federal style by John McComb, Jr., and Joseph Mangin, the structure was built in 1812. City Hall's south facade and sides were of marble, the north facade being of brownstone because it was thought no one would view it from the rear. The original building included a bell tower above the north wall which was destroyed in a fire that swept across the top of the building on August 18, 1858. The building was boarded up for some time while the roof, cupola and interior were restored. On April 24 and 25 of the year in which the Anthonys took this view, President Lincoln's body lay in state in the building. The plot of land on which it rose was all that was left of the Commons of Dutch colonial days.

34. Stewart's Dry Goods Store, Broadway and Chambers Street, 1860; E. Anthony. The large building is the store of A. T. Stewart. Having come to New York in 1823 as a 20-year-old graduate of Trinity College, Dublin, Stewart got into the dry-goods business only to redeem money loaned to a friend. He became so successful that he was able to have this beautiful building erected for his store in 1845. It was Stewart's move here that first diverted the flow of business from Chatham Street and The Bowery. In 1862, Stewart sold this building and opened a new one at Broadway and East 10th Street (see No. 62). The old building eventually had two more stories added to it and was converted for office use.

35. West side of Broadway, north from City Hall Park, ca. 1887; publisher unknown. In this view, taken about 27 years after the previous one, the horsecar has finally made its appearance on Broadway, legal battles having delayed its advent until 1885. In 1893, cars pulled by underground cables replaced the horse-powered ones.

36. Broadway, south from Duane Street, 1860; E. Anthony. This fine instantaneous view, taken about noon, shows ladies on their shopping rounds. Later in the afternoon, more leisurely promenading was enjoyed. In general, the "wrong" side of Broadway was the east side (left), which had fewer fine shops. So the ladies tended to promenade on the west side while men with cigars were expected to stay on the east side. The view extends down to the spire of Trinity Church.

37. Broadway on a rainy day, 1860. E. Anthony.
This photograph was a virtuosic show-off item,
demonstrating the ability of the Anthonys to make
instantaneous pictures even when the sky was
cloudy and the light poor. Building materials are
piled out in the street and on the sidewalk, creating
additional havoc on the already chaotic thoroughfare.

38. Broadway, north from White Street, 1880; E. & H. T. Anthony & Co. By 1880 buildings with stone or cast-iron fronts had replaced many of the older structures north of City Hall. The retail stores of the 1860s, with awnings projecting over the sidewalk, had been largely crowded out by wholesale establishments. One of the omnibus drivers rides without an umbrella in the heat, but the driver he has just passed, and many others, are using them.

39. Broadway, south from the corner of Canal Street, 1867; E. & H. T. Anthony & Co. Once again, construction materials create an obstacle to vehicles and pedestrians alike. Construction was constant on Broadway, and sometimes buildings were thrown up in such haste and with such shoddy workmanship that they collapsed.

40.   Broadway, north from the corner of Canal Street, ca. 1866; E. & H. T. Anthony & Co. The firm of Cochran & Co. specialized in laces, as did Martin & Morrison, whose far smaller shingle hangs from the awning in the foreground. An oft quoted motto of the times was "competition is the life of trade."

41. **Broadway, south from above Howard Street, ca. 1866; E. & H. T. Anthony & Co.** This view radiates with the light of a very clear New York day. The name of the Tontine Hotel recalls the well-known Tontine Coffee House of earlier times. (A tontine was a cooperative annuity whose members shared the annuity of all the members who predeceased them.)

42. Broadway, north toward Grand Street, ca. 1865; George W. Thorne. The imposing white marble building is Lord & Taylor, which had moved its business from Catherine Street to the corner of Broadway and Grand Street in 1859. The building was the last word in luxury. Its form, that of an Italian palazzo, was frequently emulated by cast-iron buildings. The view also includes the large sign of the Broadway Theatre, which was illuminated by a light within it at night. (The theater burned down early in 1866.) A bookshop can be seen across the street, but overall New York was regarded as deficient in the number of bookshops for a city of its size.

43. Broadway, north from below Howard Street, 1880; E. & H. T. Anthony & Co. As the sign near the top of the view indicates, ready-made clothing was gradually winning more acceptance and becoming more important in the city's economy.

44. The return of the New York 69th Regiment, N.Y.S.N.G., 1861; E. & H. T. Anthony & Co. This is one of the very few pictures reflecting the impact of the Civil War on New York. It was taken north of Broome Street on July 27, 1861, when the 69th Regiment of light infantry returned to the city after having completed its first front-line tour of duty, and was cheered by Irish men and women who lined Broadway. The 69th Regiment, along with the 63rd and 88th, comprised the "Irish Brigade" that was sponsored by Archbishop Hughes. It later won fame for its bravery at Bull Run and other battles. Italian and German units were also formed in the city.

45. Broadway, north from between Grand and Broome Streets, 1859; E. Anthony. The source of so many of our pictures, the E. & H. T. Anthony Co., had its offices and store in the building bearing its sign, at 501 Broadway. The company later moved to 591 Broadway.

46. Broadway, north from the corner of Broome Street, 1866; E. & H. T. Anthony & Co. The Anthonys took a fair number of pictures of Broadway from the windows and roof of their own building. In this view, just visible at the far right, is Henry Wood's Theatre, which opened in 1862 as Wood's Minstrel Hall. Owned by the brother of mayor Fernando Wood, the Tammany leader whose administration was riddled with corruption, the theater presented legitimate drama in 1866, later changed hands and was finally torn down in 1881. Perhaps the most famous name to grace its stage was the team of Harrigan and Hart.

47.   The St. Nicholas Hotel, ca. 1866; E. & H. T. Anthony & Co. Looking south on Broadway from Spring Street to Broome, we see the St. Nicholas Hotel, named after a saint especially dear to the old Dutch families of New York and opened in 1853. This hotel (which had 1000 beds), the Prescott House and the Metropolitan Hotel were all built in a spurt of expansion between 1850 and 1853.

48. Broadway, north from the corner of Spring Street, 1860; E. Anthony. This view captures New York in transition. To the far left are two of the old dormered Federal structures that housed New York's more prosperous families in the previous generation. Next to them rise new commercial structures— the city is already beginning to grow upwards. The few trees visible, remnants of more leisurely days along Broadway, are soon to fall. In this year newspapers made note that the residential enclave of Bond Street, a few blocks north of this site, had fallen to the advance of commerce.

49. The Interior of Helmbold's Drug Store, Broadway, ca. 1875; publisher unknown. Very few of the interiors of the stores that catered to the wealthy shoppers on Broadway were satisfactorily photographed. It is hard to believe that these magnificent chandeliers and opulent details were not in a jewelry or fur emporium, but in a drugstore.

50. Broadway, north from the balcony of the Metropolitan Hotel, 1860; E. Anthony. St. Thomas' Church, seen at the northwest corner of Broadway and Houston Street, was built in 1826, when this part of Broadway and the streets to the east and west were lined with fine residences. It burned in 1851 but was rebuilt the following year. Six years after this view was taken, it was sold, a new St. Thomas' was built at Fifth Avenue and 53rd Street (see No. 116) and the old building was demolished. The Metropolitan Hotel, between Prince and Houston Streets, was built in front of Niblo's Garden, which retained an entrance on Broadway.

51. Broadway, between Prince and Houston Streets, 1880. E. & H. T. Anthony & Co. This photograph was taken from the same vantage point as No. 50. St. Thomas' Church has been replaced by the structure on which the letters DEL can be seen. All the trees have vanished, replaced by a forest of utility poles. Most of the older buildings have also fallen to progress. The old omnibuses, however, continue to lumber up and down the street.

52. **Broadway, south from Houston Street, ca. 1868. E. & H. T. Anthony & Co.** Ebenezer Butterick, "reporter of fashions and patterns" and inventor of the paper clothing pattern, had only recently moved from his downtown location to the building at the middle of the block across the street when this picture was taken.

53. Broadway, south from Houston Street, ca. 1870; E. & H. T. Anthony & Co. Here is another example of the non-instantaneous photographs of later years. The panorama from a rooftop em- phasizes the variety of cornices (most of pressed metal) and shows other details not usually noticed from the street, such as the eagle, top right, and what appears to a north-light studio at the left.

54. Broadway, north from Houston Street, ca. 1866; E. & H. T. Anthony & Co. This image demonstrates the delicate balance of equipment and technique essential for obtaining high-quality instantaneous photographs on a wet plate. The photographer captured exceptionally sharp images of fairly rapidly moving traffic in the foreground, but, to do this, he had to use a wide-open lens, which cost him sharpness on more distant objects.

55. Laying the Nicolson pavement on Mercer Street, ca. 1867; E. & H. T. Anthony & Co. Streets parallel to Broadway were almost never photographed, but the Anthonys had Mercer Street taken while a new pavement, called Nicolson, was being laid. The city tried many different surfaces, in-cluding traditional cobblestones, Belgian block, Reuss block, hemlock block over two layers of crushed stone, and asphalt, to see what would hold up best. Although there was a police station on it, Mercer Street, along with Greene Street, was notorious for its "infamous resorts."

56. Grand procession in commemoration of the treaty of peace between Germany and France, 1871; E. & H. T. Anthony & Co. This picture, evidently taken from the new building of the Anthonys at 591 Broadway, shows a parade on April 10 that was probably sponsored primarily by the city's large German population. (It was Germany that had won the Franco-Prussian War.) The French population of New York, though significant in terms of cultural contributions, was far smaller. The solar printers on the roof top across the street appear to be enlargers utilizing sunlight. Two buildings beyond the Museum of Anatomy is the Olympic Theatre (see No. 57).

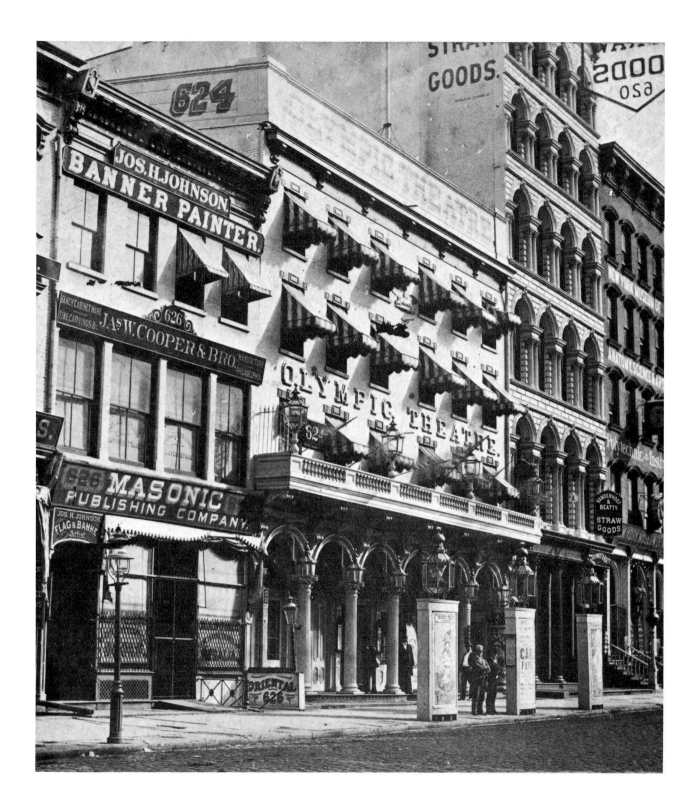

57. The Olympic Theatre, ca. 1875, publisher unknown. Here is a close-up of the Olympic Theatre, opened 1856 and originally known as "Laura Keene's." It became the Olympic in 1866 under Mrs. John Wood, but passed to other hands.

In 1868, the great pantomime *Humpty Dumpty*, with George L. Fox and Charles F. Fox, opened here and ran for 483 performances and another 333 in a revival. The theater was torn down in 1880.

58. Broadway between Bleecker and West 3rd Streets, ca. 1880; publisher unknown. As we approach the Astor Place neighborhood, businesses dedicated to the printed word, such as newspapers, printers and bookbinders, become evident. Pfaff's, the hangout of the "Bohemians," was in the basement of the third building from the corner. Among the famous who were seen there were Ada Isaacs Menken, Walt Whitman, Lola Montez and William Dean Howells. In the far distance is Grace Church.

59. The Grand Central Hotel, ca. 1870; E. & H. T. Anthony & Co. The Grand Central Hotel, opened on August 25, 1875 on Broadway between Bleecker and West 3rd Streets, was a "monster edifice" for its time. It had been erected for E. S. Higgens, a carpet manufacturer, who wished to have the most palatial hotel in America. In fact, with 630 rooms on eight stories and a marble front topped with a mansard roof, it was the largest in the world. On Janary 6, 1872, on the stairway leading from the office to the second floor, capitalist and bon vivant Col. Jim Fisk was shot to death by Edward Stokes, his rival for the heart of Josie Mansfield. The name of the hotel was later changed to the Broadway Central. The building, sleazy and long since stripped of any remainder of opulence, collapsed into Broadway in the early 1970s.

60. Broadway from below Great Jones Street, ca. 1880; publisher unknown. This view, taken from the balcony of the Grand Central Hotel, shows the retail shopping center of the 1880s, with the great A. T. Stewart store (see No. 62) visible to the right of Grace Church in the distance.

61. **Broadway, north from the corner of Astor Place, ca. 1865; E. & H. T. Anthony & Co.** This section of Broadway had art and auction galleries a century ago; similar establishments are found there today.

62. **A. T. Stewart's Retail Store, Broadway and East 10th Street, ca. 1869; E. & H. T. Anthony & Co.** This, the store that Stewart had built when he left Chambers Street, was the largest retail store in the city when it was completed in 1859. Designed by John W. Kellum, the building was constructed of cast-iron painted gray and olive green. Stewart's foresight in moving north was soon justified, as this store became the anchor for a string of fine retail shops for women's goods that ran to 23rd Street.

63. The bend in Broadway at Grace Church, 1880; E. & H. T. Anthony & Co. Broadway makes a sharp bend at 11th Street, where Grace Church is located. The church, designed by James Renwick and built of white marble in 1845, is one of the most beautiful ecclesiastic structures in the United States. It was supported by the many wealthy families who lived in brownstone and brick mansions clustered around Fifth Avenue and Union Square. "Boss" Tweed once threatened to run 11th Street through the church and its grounds, but discreetly backed off. In 1863 Charles Stratton (better known as P. T. Barnum's star attraction, General Tom Thumb) married another midget, Lavinia Warren Bumpus, in a greatly publicized ceremony that must have contrasted sharply with the sedate society weddings that were more customary in the church.

64. Broadway, north toward East 11th Street, ca. 1887; publisher unknown. The structure in the distance, with a flag flying from its cupola, was the Domestic Sewing Machine Company's building on Union Square. The tallest building in the city when it was constructed in 1872–73, it was a favorite subject of the Anthonys. The imposing white edifice on the far side of East 11th Street, with mansard roof and flagpole, is the James McCreery department store, erected in 1868. A notable example of cast-iron architecture, it still stands, having been converted to luxury housing. On the near side of East 11th Street, also with a flagpole, is the Hotel St. Denis. Built in 1848 and renovated in 1875, it was one of the city's leading hotels and housed, among others, Abraham Lincoln, U.S. Grant and Sarah Bernhardt. In 1877, in one of the hotel's rooms, Alexander Graham Bell demonstrated the telephone in New York. The building survives, although stripped of all architectural detail.

65. Wallack's Theatre, ca. 1867; E. & H. T. Anthony & Co. A famous building across the street and a few doors south of the Domestic Sewing Machine Company was Wallack's Theatre. It was built for James Wallack at the northeast corner of 13th Street in 1861. Lester Wallack, who soon took over the management, posed in his carriage for this picture. He tried to maintain the best stock company in the United States and to establish his theater as the leader in comedy in the city. In 1881, when his theater was the only one on Broadway south of 23rd Street, he bowed to the times and moved to 30th Street and Broadway.

66. East along 14th Street from the Domestic Sewing Company Building, ca. 1872; E. & H. T. Anthony & Co. At the center of the photograph, the German Savings Bank, designed by Henry Fernbach, is nearing completion. Across 14th Street, on the corner of Irving Place, is the Academy of Music (see No. 71). Farther down the block and adjacent to the Academy is Tammany Hall (see No. 72).

**67. East side of Union Square, ca. 1869; E. &
H. T. Anthony & Co.** This view, also taken from
the Domestic Sewing Machine Company building,
leaves no doubt that the heart of the musical life of
the city was in the Union Square section in the
1860s. Three of the buildings are packed with
dealers in pianos, piano stools and organs, and a
music academy. Schirmer and Ditson & Co. were
also in the area for many years.

68. The Washington Statue in Union Square, ca. 1871; publisher unknown. Henry Kirke Brown's masterful equestrian statue of Washington, one of the earliest pieces of civic sculpture in the city, was unveiled in 1856. A "slave market" for unemployed actors met near the statue in summer, waiting for possible employers. A miscellaneous group of gamins pose for the photographer at the base of the statue.

69. Fourth Avenue, north from Union Square, ca. 1871; publisher unknown. Union Square was a rallying point for patriotic and political events, such as the great Union Meeting held here at the start of the Civil War. At the time this picture was taken, a now-forgotten politician was making his appeal to the people. In later years, anarchists and other radicals were more likely to be heard making speeches in the park. The building at the end of the square, at the left of this view, is the Everett House (see No. 76).

70. Steinway & Sons' Piano Warerooms, East 14th Street, ca. 1864; E. & H. T. Anthony & Co. Just off Union Square was Steinway Hall, which housed a theater for musical and "other reputable entertainments." Its auditorium, which had an organ built into it, seated over 1,800 people.

71. The Academy of Music, East 14th Street and Irving Place, ca. 1875; publisher unknown. This theater, the first in New York that succeeded in presenting regular seasons of grand opera, was opened on October 2, 1854 with a performance of Bellini's *Norma*. The house burned in 1866, but was reopened two years later. Its plain exterior belied the attractive decoration inside. The building also accommodated fashionable balls (such as that given for the Prince of Wales in 1860) and amateur theatrical performances. The Academy of Music lost out to the competition the Metropolitan Opera offered when it opened in 1883. The theater was converted for use by straight theatrical productions and was eventually demolished.

72. Tammany Hall and Bryant's Theatre, East 14th Street, ca. 1875; publisher unknown. Founded in 1789, the New York Tammany Society was a moving force in politics throughout the nineteenth century. This, the Society's third meeting place (or Wigwam), was opened in 1868. A statue of its sachem stands on the cornice. Bryant's Theatre occupied a part of the building; its entrance is at the left. In 1881 the theater was taken over by Tony Pastor, who ran it as a variety hall with great success until his death in 1908. Among the celebrities with whom he was associated were Weber and Fields, Lillian Russell and Marie Lloyd.

73. Tiffany & Co.'s Store, ca. 1870; E. & H. T. Anthony & Co. On the west side of Union Square was Henry Kirke Brown's statue of Lincoln (1866), seen in the lower left corner of this picture. Behind is the Spingler House, whose name derives from the Spingler farm that once occupied 22 acres between 14th and 16th Streets, west of Bowery Road. Next to it, on 15th Street, is the Tiffany Building, whose architecture received the following uncomplimentary criticism: "heavy and ungainly cast iron postbellum style." Tiffany moved there from Broadway and Broome in 1870, and remained until 1905.

74.   The west side of Union Square, looking south down Broadway, 1860. E. & H. T. Anthony & Co. The Tiffany building stands at the corner of East 15th Street. Next to it, with a pediment, is the Spingler Building, built in 1872 on the site of the Spingler House. It was destroyed by fire in 1893. Note the hackstand at the left.

75. The west side of Union Square, looking north up Broadway, 1880; E. & H. T. Anthony & Co. In this view we are looking up what was known as the "Ladies' Mile," although it was actually only the nine blocks from 14th Street to 23rd Street. From about 1880 to 1900, the concentration of luxury shops for women in this stretch was unequaled anywhere in the United States.

76. The northeast corner of Union Square, ca. 1870; E. & H. T. Anthony & Co. In the early 1860s the square and its environs were a most fashionable neighborhood. By the time this photograph was taken, however, commercial establishments were beginning to make inroads — notice the house on the northeast corner of Fourth Avenue and East 17th Street that bears the sign "Slatework." Although most wealthier residents had moved farther north by 1880, the park was still frequented by nurse-maids and their little charges. The large building facing the park is the Everett House, built in 1854. On special occasions, the street in front of it was lighted by ornamental colored gas lamps. Farther up Fourth Avenue, at East 20th Street, marked by its dome, is the All Souls' Unitarian Church (see No. 101).

77. Lord & Taylor's Store, Broadway and East 20th Street, ca. 1875; C. W. Woodward, Rochester, N.Y. In 1873 Lord & Taylor moved from their marble palace on Broadway and Grand Street to this Second-Empire cast-iron building, designed by James H. Giles. Here the business flourished until it moved to its present store in 1914. Lord & Taylor's was one of the principal stores along the "Ladies' Mile," the others being Arnold Constable at East 19th Street and J. & C. Johnston at East 22nd Street. The Broadway blocks north of East 23rd Street catered to men.

78. Broadway and East 22nd Street, looking north, ca. 1880; Continent Stereoscopic Co. Where Broadway's diagonal path crossed north-south avenues, triangular blocks resulted. Enterprising developers made their buildings fit the irregular plots, as seen here in the old St. Germain Hotel (1855), later renamed the Cumberland Apartments.

The city would be amazed when the famous 22-story Fuller Building, better known as the Flat-iron Building, rose on the triangle in 1902. A similar course was taken when the Times Tower rose on the triangular island in Times Square. In the distance, far right, is the Fifth Avenue Hotel.

79.   The Fifth Avenue Hotel, ca. 1887; publisher unknown. Amos R. Enos opened his opulent six-story hotel on the west side of Fifth Avenue between 23rd and 24th Streets, in 1859. This 800-bed establishment boasted one of the first passenger elevators in the city, many private bathrooms, and luxurious public rooms. For many years *the* hotel at which to stay in New York, it was demolished in 1908. This view was taken shortly before the telegraph and telephone wires were laid underground in conduits in 1889.

80. The Worth Monument, Madison Square, ca. 1880; publisher unknown. We are looking south toward the juncture of Fifth Avenue and Broadway. The 51-foot obelisk marks the grave of Major-General Worth. A gallant soldier of the War of 1812 and of the Seminole and Mexican campaigns, Worth died in Texas in 1849, but his body was brought to New York in 1857 to lie in state in City Hall and to be interred here. At the far right is the Albemarle Hotel, favored by English visitors to the city. Across West 24th Street is the Fifth Avenue Hotel.

81. Jim Fisk's Grand Opera House, ca. 1875; John S. Moulton, Salem, Mass. Samuel N. Pike thought he could give the Academy of Music a run for its money when he opened this opera house at Eighth Avenue and West 23rd Street on January 9, 1868, with a performance of *Il Trovatore.* The Academy's audience remained loyal, and the next year Pike sold the building to Col. James Fisk and Jay Gould, who ran the theater and operated the Erie Railroad from offices in the upper stories. Even in an era when shady practices among capitalists were run of the mill, the strategies of Fisk and Gould scandalized the public. They are perhaps best remembered for the Black Friday they precipitated in their attempt to corner the gold market in September, 1869. When Fisk was killed in 1872, his body lay in state in the opera house. Thereafter, the theater had a checkered career, including use for vaudeville and motion pictures. It burned in 1960.

82.   Chatham Square, 1860; George W. Thorne.
Chatham Square once rivaled Broadway as a shopping center. It remained one of the busiest spots in
the city, especially for working people.

83. Chatham Square, looking up The Bowery, ca. 1865; publisher unknown. The square was a center of transportation. About a half-dozen horsecar lines traversed it and it was later covered by the shadow of three branches of the elevated railroad. The principal hack stand for the East Side was also located in the square.

84.   Chatham Square, looking up The Bowery, ca. 1870. E. & H. T. Anthony. This view, taken later than No. 83 and more northerly in direction, shows the turnover in business in a city of unbounded opportunities to succeed — or fail.

85. **Looking up East Broadway from the corner of New Bowery, ca. 1866; E. & H. T. Anthony & Co.** The most intriguing detail in this view is the sign for "Cooper's Glue by the Barrel at his Prices." From such mundane material, made in a superior way, Peter Cooper gained the capital to invest in a wide range of ventures and used his wealth to enhance the city's cultural and educational life (see No. 99).

86. Canal Street, west from Mulberry Street, ca. 1870; E. & H. T. Anthony & Co. Canal Street had a more exotic flavor than Broadway, as neighborhoods populated by various national or racial minorities clustered around it. Orientals were not unusual there, and part of Thompson Street, just north of Canal, was called "Africa," as it was almost completely black.

87. Five Points, ca. 1875; publisher unknown.
The "Five Points," strictly speaking, were the intersection of Park, Worth and Baxter Streets, where a swampy area of Manhattan had been developed for the poor. Though it was only a few blocks west of Chatham Square, the Five Points neighborhood held the worst slums of the city, including the notorious "Old Brewery" and other "rookeries" where people, packed together in decrepit and filthy buildings, toted up staggering annual records of altercations, murders, robberies and other crimes. Very few photographs were taken in these streets, as it was unsafe for a stranger, even without an expensive camera, to venture upon them.

**88.   The Five Points Mission, ca. 1875; non-stereo-
scopic view, Bogardus Gallery.** Efforts to clean up
the Five Points began in 1850, when the Five Points
Mission was established. In 1852 it built this structure on the site of the infamous Old Brewery. By the
1870s the area was becoming somewhat tamer and
cleaner thanks to the Rev. Lewis Morris Pease and
others who risked their lives in doing mission work
in the area. They took responsibility for the up-
bringing, education and training of abandoned
children, and also worked with adults in trouble.
Italians and Chinese immigrants settled in the area
and stabilized it, but there remained some residents
of the old type who dealt in stolen goods.

89. A load of immigrants, ca. 1895; publisher unknown. This group is in transit, possibly off to a new place of employment in the city, possibly to a station to board a train and continue out West. By the 1890s, high-speed dry plates and film, used in lighter and more compact cameras, made it much easier to take candid photographs of this type in all parts of the city.

90. A street in the tenement district, ca. 1900; publisher unknown. Although tenements such as these, laid out on the "railroad flat" plan with inadequate light and ventilation, came in time to be condemned, they were nevertheless superior to what they replaced — subdivided mansions, abandoned years earlier by the rich, which were in a shocking state of decay. At least the average tenement had fire escapes and was, by comparison, more comfortable and commodious.

91. A New York street organ, ca. 1895; publisher unknown. For many of the poor, the only source of music was the street organ, which poured out popular songs and snatches of opera. The organ-grinder subsisted on the few pennies children brought him from their parents, or which were thrown down to him from upstairs windows, wrapped in a piece of paper.

92. Candy man in Hester Street, ca. 1895; publisher unknown. Hester Street was a major thoroughfare in the large Jewish section of the Lower East Side. Though most of the families were poor, a penny could be found to allow a child to buy a surprising amount of candy from the candy man.

483a Ice Cream.

93. Ice cream cart, ca. 1895; publisher unknown.
Vendors of ice cream and ices were very popular in the summer months, when the temperature soared and there were no air-conditioned movies to provide temporary relief. The vendors' wares might not have been very sanitary, but no one minded. With as little as a penny you could have a small paper cup filled with cooling ice cream.

94. Odd Fellow's Hall, corner of Centre and Grand Streets, ca. 1865; publisher unknown. As one moved uptown on the East Side, the social environment changed from poor to middle class and finally to upper class. The Odd Fellow's, for example, was essentially a middle-class organization, akin to the Masons, and its Grand Lodge for the Southern New York District met in this handsome building (erected in 1849) four times a year. The "Grand Encampment" was held in it twice a year. Considerably altered, it still stands.

95. Tony Pastor's Opera House, 201 The Bowery, 1865–75, publisher unknown. Tony Pastor, who came from a threatrical family, appeared for a while on stage himself, and then operated a series of theaters including this, at 201 The Bowery, which he ran in partnership with Sam Sharpley from 1865 until 1875.

96. The Astor Library, Lafayette Place, ca. 1865, E. & H. T. Anthony & Co. A codicil in the will of John Jacob Astor provided the funds that enabled the library to be started. It was constructed in three stages: the first (right) was completed in 1853; the central section (left) was completed in 1859; the north wing was not built until 16 years after this photograph was taken. Although not a lending library, the institution was free and open to all. Since it had no artificial lighting, it had to close at sunset. It had a capacity of half a million books and reached an actual figure of about 222,000 by the end of 1885. In 1895 the Astor Library, the Lenox Library and the Tilden Trust merged to create the New York Public Library. Today this building houses the New York Shakespeare Festival Public Theatre.

97. Lafayette Place, north from Great Jones Street, ca. 1866; E. & H. T. Anthony & Co. This rare view captures the charm of elegant streets that had been tastefully planned by old New York's leading families. (In the 1860s it took a previous three generations of gentility to establish a family's credentials.) Lafayette Place (graced by Colonnade Row), as well as Second Avenue, preserved its status long after the advance of commerce drove almost all the residences of "upper crust" society from Broadway. But it could hold out only for a while. By 1902 the street had been extended and renamed Lafayette Street, and all the trees in this view had been cut down.

98. Seventh Regiment Armory, Third Avenue and East 6th Street, ca. 1867; E. & H. T. Anthony & Co. Farther up the East Side was this building, titled on different stereographs as the Armory or as Tompkins Market. The first floor was, indeed, devoted to a market which spilled over into oyster stands on the sidewalk. The rest of the structure (erected in 1860) was used for the Seventh Regi- ment's activities. The second and third floors were taken up by armories and drill and meeting rooms. The basement was employed for target practice and squad drill. The building with the mansard roof on East 7th Street (left) is the Metropolitan Savings Bank, built in 1867 as one of the city's earliest fire- proof structures.

99.   **Cooper Union, ca. 1866; E. & H. T. Anthony & Co.** Cooper Union was built one block north of Tompkins Market in 1859. It had been founded in 1857 by Peter Cooper to furnish free education for persons employed during the day, and remains a prestigious educational asset of the city. Its Great Hall became a meeting place where new ideas in politics, social reform and religion were heard. It is most famous as the scene of Lincoln's 1860 "might makes right" speech which established him as a leading Republican candidate for the Presidency. Like many other buildings not fully employed every day (see No. 94), Cooper Union paid part of its expenses with the rents of stores built into the ground floor — a type of combined use that helped make the city street active and interesting.

100. New York, Harlem & Albany Railroad Company Depot, ca. 1865; George W. Thorne. In 1863, when 14th Street was still considered the probable limit of intensive development of the city, the railroad built its depot on the block bounded by East 26th and 27th Streets and Madison and Fourth Avenues. Trains ran on surface tracks north along Fourth Avenue. The company ran horsecars south from the depot to The Bowery and from there down to the Astor House. In 1873, the year after the railroad set up a new station at 42nd Street, P. T. Barnum leased the building, using it as a place of public amusements. In 1879 it was renamed Madison Square Garden. It was demolished in 1889, to make way for Stanford White's magnificent new Madison Square Garden.

101. All Souls Unitarian Church, ca. 1866; E. & H. T. Anthony & Co. The architecture of churches and temples built in New York from the 1850s on was far more imaginative than that of most other buildings. The All Souls Unitarian Church, at Fourth Avenue and 20th Street, is believed to have been the first edifice of Byzantine style in the city. It was built in 1855 after designs by J. W. Mould, of Caen stone and red brick. A statue of Dr. Henry W. Bellows, its pastor, sculpted by Augustus Saint-Gaudens, was later placed within it.

102.   The Free Academy, ca. 1866; E. & H. T. Anthony & Co. Opened in 1849 at the corner of Lexington Avenue and East 23rd Street, the institution changed its name to the College of the City of New York in 1866. At first it educated young men in a curriculum in the standard classical mold, but later added courses in science and postgraduate engineering.

**103. The National Academy of Design, ca. 1868;
E. & H. T. Anthony & Co.** By the time this photograph was taken, soon after the 1865 opening of the impressive structure on East 23rd Street and Fourth Avenue, the National Academy of Design had gained recognition as the foremost art institution in the country for its galleries and free courses. The Academy had been formed in 1826 by a group of 30 artists, led by Samuel F. B. Morse. It had many difficult years before it accumulated the finances that allowed it to build this palazzo of gray and white marble and bluestone in the Venetian Gothic style. It was demolished in 1899.

104. The Union League Club, ca. 1869; E. & H. T. Anthony & Co. This imposing building at the corner of East 26th Street and Madison Avenue was built in 1859 as the residence of Leonard Jerome, maternal grandfather of Winston Churchill. By the time this view was taken, it had become the home of the Union League Club, which had been formed in the early years of the Civil War, following a Philadelphia model, to help the government raise troops. Its membership for many years was restricted to Republicans and it gradually tended to be composed of older men. The New York Club was its counterpart for the younger men of similar political philosophy. The building was later occupied by the University Club and the Manhattan Club. It was demolished in 1966.

105. East 26th Street, west from Madison Avenue, ca. 1868; E. & H. T. Anthony & Co. As the number of affluent New Yorkers increased after the Civil War, single-family "brownstones" were built in rows such as this to accommodate them. The design became more or less standardized, with a high stoop to the first floor. Considered a New York innovation, it was soon copied elsewhere.

106. Stewart's Home for Women, ca. 1878; G. W. Pach. The view looks south to the cast-iron edifice, designed by John Kellum and opened in 1878 on Park Avenue between 32nd and 33rd Streets as a hotel at which young ladies could reside without endangering their virtue. The rates were so high however, and the restrictions so stringent, that the business soon failed. The building was reopened as the Park Avenue Hotel. It was demolished in 1927. In the foreground are cars on the tracks of the New York & Harlem Railroad.

107. Church of the Messiah, ca. 1869; E. & H. T. Anthony & Co. The Unitarians chose this striking design, influenced by French medieval architecture, for the structure built at Fourth Avenue and 34th Street in 1867.

108. West 34th Street, from Fifth Avenue, ca. 1866; E. & H. T. Anthony & Co. Some of the brownstones were often sold ready-made to families with incomes of $5,000 a year or more. The developers who engaged in this building sometimes lured inexperienced buyers by putting extra money into fancy exterior decoration while skimping on basics such as plumbing. Potential buyers often did better by constructing their own homes. In the distance is the Broadway Tabernacle Church on Sixth Avenue, constructed in 1859 and torn down in 1905.

109. Residence of A. T. Stewart, northwest corner of 34th Street and Fifth Avenue, ca. 1870; E. & H. T. Anthony & Co. Builders occasionally constructed large mansions on speculation for sale to the nouveau riche, but wiser men of wealth preferred to contract for exactly what they wanted. A. T. Stewart had his "Marble Palace" built on the site of the home of Dr. "Sarsaparilla" Townsend. It was finished in 1869; Stewart lived there only seven years until his death in 1876. His widow survived him by ten years. After her death the building housed the Manhattan Club. It was demolished in 1903.

110. 38th Street, east from Fifth Avenue, ca. 1866; E. & H. T. Anthony & Co. All the blocks north of Union Square were considered to be the "acme of fashion" in the 1860s, and many churches of different sects were built as the blocks filled up with brownstones. The structure at Madison Avenue in this photograph is the Zion Protestant Episcopal Church. In 1890, it was sold and became the South Reformed Dutch Church.

111. Fourth Avenue and East 34th Street, ca. 1864; E. & H. T. Anthony & Co. This is the Murray Hill section of the city. The tracks of the Harlem Railroad ran beneath Fourth Avenue at this point.

The owner of the Gothic Revival mansion on the corner has held out against the row developers. As a result, the brownstone on the left has a rare feature: a bay of windows on a wall that is usually blank.

112. Temple Emanu-El, Fifth Avenue and East 43rd Street, ca. 1870; E. & H. T. Anthony & Co. This impressive structure, designed by Leopold Eidlitz in the Moorish style, had been open for only two years when this view was taken. It had been constructed of brown and yellow sandstone with a roof of alternate lines of red and black tiles at a cost of $60,000. The auditorium sat 2,000. Because of the increasing value of the land on which the temple stood, the site was sold and the building demolished in 1927. The present temple Emanu-El stands at Fifth Avenue and East 65th Street.

113. **East 42nd Street, opposite Grand Central Terminal, 1893; Strohmeyer & Wyman.** The construction, in 1871, of the Grand Central Terminal at East 42nd Street to serve the New York Central and New York & New Haven Railroads made 42nd Street a major crosstown road, with all sorts of transportation converging on it, including a spur of the elevated railroad.

114. **The Windsor Hotel, ca. 1880; publisher unknown.** The center of the wealthy residential neighborhoods moved north and new hotels followed. The 500-room Windsor Hotel, covering two-thirds of an acre, ran between East 46th and 47th Streets on Fifth Avenue. Built in 1873, it was destroyed by fire with the loss of about 20 lives in 1899. At the right is the Church of the Heavenly Rest.

115. 49th Street, west from Fifth Avenue, ca. 1875; publisher unknown. This is one of the rela- tively few buildings that broke the brownstone pat- terns in the side streets.

116. The Vanderbilt Mansions, Fifth Avenue, ca. 1884; E. & H. T. Anthony & Co. The wealth of the Vanderbilts allowed them to occupy whole block fronts on Fifth Avenue. Perhaps most famous of all the mansions were the twin brownstones erected by W. H. Vanderbilt in 1880–84. The northernmost of the pair, seen at the left, was occupied by his sons-in-law, Elliott F. Shepard and William D. Sloane.

To the right, across West 52nd Street, is the French chateau style mansion built by Richard Morris Hunt of Indiana limestone in 1879–81 for W. K. Vanderbilt. Mr. W. K. Vanderbilt, Jr., later built a house adjoining that one. The tower far right is part of St. Thomas's Church at West 53rd Street. Destroyed by fire in 1905, it was replaced by the present edifice.

117. **Fifth Avenue near 59th Street, ca. 1870; E. & H. T. Anthony & Co.** These buildings foretell the profusion of ornate and elegant architectural designs that would flower on the avenue and on side streets north of 59th Street. At the far right we have typical brownstones. Next to them are two structures with mansard roofs in the French Second-Empire style. Then follow residences in the Italianate style, with pediments over the windows and a balustrade atop the cornice. Closing the view is a Gothic Revival structure. The blank wall emphasizes the fact that all these styles were mere dressings for these structures — that "under the skin" they bore great similarity.

118.   **Third Avenue Railroad Depot, ca. 1867. E. & H. T. Anthony & Co.** The Third Avenue Railroad anticipated the expansion of the city better than most other transit companies when it built this car barn "away up town" at East 65th Street. In 1870, cars left the barn at three-quarter minute intervals during rush hours, and at one-minute intervals the rest of the day. Even so, cars in rush hours were often heavily overloaded, placing a severe strain on the horses. The Third Avenue Railroad required 1,600 horses, 250 cars, and 1,000 men to maintain its schedule.

119. **Old Men and Women's Hospital, Lenox Hill, ca. 1872; E. & H. T. Anthony & Co.** Hospitals, asylums and other agencies also went north where large plots of land at reasonable cost were still obtainable. This particular hospital, endowed by James Lenox and built in 1872, was later called the Presbyterian Hospital.

120. N.Y. Central and Harlem Railroad Freight Depot, ca. 1871; publisher unknown. The lower West Side had fewer points of interest than the East Side, but one imposing if not artistic structure there was the large freight depot erected in 1867 by the N.Y. Central and Hudson River Railroad Company on the site of St. John's Park. It drove out the residents for whom the park had been an exclusive enclave since St. John's Chapel had been built in 1803. The one feature of the depot that attracted special attention was its colossal pediment, known as the Vanderbilt Bronzes.

121. The Vanderbilt Bronzes, ca. 1871; E. & H. T. Anthony & Co. Located on the Hudson Street side of the depot, the bronzes had a design that celebrated Commodore Vanderbilt's colorful and successful career in organizing great ocean steam- ship lines and railroads. It was completed in 1869. The 17-foot statue of the Commodore by Albert DeGroot now stands at the head of the downtown entrance to the auto ramps that encircle Grand Central Terminal.

122. The American Express Building, Hudson Street, ca. 1867; E. & H. T. Anthony & Co. The birth of the American Express Company was brought about by Wells, Fargo, and other pioneer expressmen. Its New York building stood along the route of the N.Y. Central & Hudson Railroad, whose freight cars, as seen here, shared the railroad's tracks with its local horsecars.

123. Manhattan Market, foot of West 34th Street, ca. 1872; E. & H. T. Anthony & Co. Large, enclosed markets, as well as outdoor pushcart markets, have fluctuated in favor in New York, depending in part on land values, shifts in populations and competitive forces. Manhattan Market, which did not survive long, had a more interesting architectural design than the usual utilitarian style.

124. The first elevated railroad, Greenwich Street, ca. 1869; National Photograph Company. Frustrating traffic jams in rush hours had encouraged the idea of elevated railroads long before this one was built by the West Side and Yonkers Patent Railway. In 1868 inventor Charles T. Harvey had built and tested a segment running along Greenwich Street from the Battery to Cortlandt Street, the cars operating on a cable. The line was opened the year this view was taken, and was extended as far as West 30th Street in 1870. The following year the line was purchased by the New York Elevated Railroad Company.

125. An elevated railroad station, ca. 1871; E. & H. T. Anthony & Co. The favorable aspects of the operation of the Greenwich Street elevated line quickly led to the construction of more lines, but with steam locomotives to move the trains. As this picture shows, the supports for the structure inter- fered with street and sidewalk traffic, darkened the streets and stores, and brought noise, smoke and a loss of privacy to tenants at the second-floor level along the route. However, the benefits to the city as a whole were deemed justification for the ills.

126.   **The Metropolitan Elevated Railroad station, Sixth Avenue and West 14th Street, ca. 1875; publisher unknown.** The Metropolitan Elevated Railroad, which controlled the Second and Sixth Avenue lines, and the Eighth and Ninth Avenue lines north of 53rd Street, had its Sixth Avenue stations built in a "Swiss chalet" style designed by landscape painter Jasper F. Cropsey. Glass with floral motifs, fanciful ironwork and other details made the stations most attractive when they were new and freshly painted.

127. The elevated railroad on The Bowery, ca. 1895; publisher unknown. The Third Avenue elevated railroad ran from South Ferry to the Harlem River, using The Bowery on its way north. The view shows one of the later types of steam locomotives. At the left, the Bowery Mission, housed in an old dormered building, offered a night's shelter for twenty-five cents. Well before the turn of the century, The Bowery had become known as the hangout for men down on their luck.

128. Central Park Garden, Seventh Avenue between West 58th and 59th Streets, ca. 1869; publisher unknown. Central Park was the primary new development of the 1860s in northern Manhattan. Just below it was the privately owned Central Park Garden, a pleasure resort at which entertainment, including orchestral music conducted by Theodore Thomas, was offered. Around 1883 the Garden became the Central Park Riding Academy, which survived until 1916.

129. Rustic arbor, Central Park, ca. 1875; J. W. & J. S. Moulton, Salem, Mass. Opened in 1858 and developed over the following years, the park was considered the finest in the world and was photographed by many galleries, some of them out of town. It accommodated many pursuits, including rest or quiet conversation in the cool shade of a rustic arbor.

130. Goat team and carriage, Central Park, ca. 1871; publisher unknown. Rides for children were a feature of the park for many years. Goat-drawn carriages, ponies and, at one time, miniature steam-engine trains were allowed to operate.

131. The camel at work, Central Park, ca. 1869; E. & H. T. Anthony & Co. Although the menagerie had not been part of Olmsted and Vaux's original plan for the park, it proved a favorite spot for children. The camel, in the years when the park was far less crowded than it is today, could be given exercise in the maintenance of the grounds.

132. The Belvedere, Central Park, ca. 1880; publisher unknown. On Vista Rock, at the highest point in the park (140.6 feet above sea level), the Romanesque castle was built in 1869. Its tiny scale was carefully contrived by Calvert Vaux to make vistas leading up to it seem longer and to increase the sense of scale in the park. Its parapets afforded superb views.

133. Interior, Mineral Springs Pavilion, Central Park, ca. 1875; publisher unknown. In 1868 this pavilion, designed by Calvert Vaux in the Gothic style, was erected by the mineral-waters firm of Schultz and Warker at their own expense. To pre-vent setting a precedent that might spread commercial development within the park, the commissioners bought the structure and ran it for many years. It was demolished in 1960, after years of neglect.

134. The Dakota Flats from Central Park, ca. 1884; E. & H. T. Anthony & Co. In this view it is easy to see how the venerable apartment building got its name: it stood in such isolation that it "might as well be in the Dakota Territory." Constructed on Central Park West and West 72nd Street in 1884 after designs by Henry J. Hardenbergh, it was one of the earliest blocks of flats that made apartment living respectable for people with considerable amounts of money. As such buildings proliferated in the 1880s, cooperatives were introduced at prices as high as $60,000 — a staggering sum in those days.

135. Fire watchtower, Mount Morris Park, ca. 1875; Continent Stereoscopic Company. In Harlem, which had been an independent hamlet not many years earlier, the most arresting landmark was the cast-iron fire watchtower in Mount Morris (now Marcus Garvey) Park. Built in 1856, it was but one of a system of such towers throughout the city which facilitated the early detection of fires.

136. **High Bridge promenade and water tower, ca. 1870; non-stereoscopic view, publisher unknown.** For a pleasant, not overly strenuous outing, some New Yorkers liked to take a horsecar, or board a Harlem River steamboat at Peck Slip, and go to High Bridge, where a promenade went across the Harlem River to Claremont. The bridge, completed in 1848, supported the large aqueducts bringing Croton water to the city. In the late 1850s a walk over the aqueducts was added. The tower beyond, on the Manhattan side of the river, held a 55,000-gallon reservoir of water to regulate the pressure for elevated sections of the city.

137. **Kingsbridge, Harlem River, ca. 1875; publisher unknown.** Broadway merged into Kingsbridge Road at 168th Street, ran north to Spuyten Duyvel Creek, crossed to the village of Kingsbridge on a bridge of the same name, and once more became Broadway. When this view was taken, the country in this area was still close to its natural state, covered by forests, a lake and creeks, among which stately old homes and mansions resisted the tides of change. However, real-estate developers were putting up modern mansions, and in 1884 the city stepped in to save more than 1,100 acres for Van Cortland Park.

138. Railroad bridge across the Harlem River, looking east, ca. 1867; E. & H. T. Anthony & Co. In addition to bridges for pedestrians and horse-drawn vehicles, there were railroad bridges crossing the Harlem River. This one, owned by the New York & Harlem Railroad, was leased to the New York and New Haven Line, which used the tracks into Manhattan.

139.   Williamsbridge, on the New York & New Haven Railroad, ca. 1867; E. & H. T. Anthony & Co. After passing through the village of Kingsbridge, Broadway continued north, becoming the Albany Post Road. Most traffic followed a fork to the east, which went to Williamsbridge and became the famous Boston Post Road. Williamsbridge was also a station on the New York & New Haven Railroad, but one of very little importance in the 1860s.

140. Street view in Williamsbridge, ca. 1868; publisher unknown. This is a very rare view of Williamsbridge when it was still a drowsy country hamlet. It had some fame as a center of a local French community, whose cuisine attracted gourmets. The western section of what is now the Bronx was part of the town of Yonkers until 1872, when it split off to become the town of Kingsbridge. New York absorbed it in 1874. It was not until 1895 that the eastern area was added to Greater New York.

141. Construction of the Brooklyn Bridge approach, non-stereoscopic view, Hall Brothers. Brooklyn very early became the "bedroom" community for thousands of people who worked in Manhattan. Some were fairly well-to-do men whose homes in Brooklyn Heights gave them a beautiful view of the harbor, but others were lower-paid professionals and working men who could not afford to live comfortably in Manhattan. Many ferries carried them across the river, but severe winters in the 1860s froze the East River or filled it with ice gorges, convincing the city of the need for a bridge to supplement the ferries. Work on the bridge, designed by John Augustus Roebling and built by his son Washington, began in January 1870, and required leveling several blocks at each end for the towers, approaches and anchorages.

142. Brooklyn Bridge tower construction, from New York Side, publisher unknown. This rare view shows the falsework on the Brooklyn tower (in the distance) and the rigs required for earlier stages of work on the Manhattan tower, which, it was found, had to be built on the bedrock of Manhattan instead of on pilings, and therefore took longer to build.

143. Brooklyn Bridge Construction, New York Side, publisher unknown. A tremendous mass of masonry was required at each side of the bridge to anchor the ends of the suspension cables. This stereograph is one of a considerable number taken to record the steps in the building of the bridge. Unfortunately, they did not have a very wide sale, and consequently are rare today.

144.   Brooklyn Bridge and the Fulton Ferry Terminal, Brooklyn Side, ca. 1885; publisher unknown. The completion of the bridge in 1883 did not end the ferry service; the Fulton Ferry continued until 1924. For many commuters it was more convenient to take a horsecar right to the ferry terminal instead of going over the bridge. The florid terminal building was constructed in 1871.

145. City Hall Fountain, Brooklyn, ca. 1868; publisher unknown. The city of Brooklyn (it did not become a borough until 1898) had almost no buildings or other sites that publishers of stereographs deemed worthy of placing in their catalogs for national distribution. However, this charming view of children watching the fountain at City Hall (itself a noteworthy building) turned out to be a popular one.

146. The Manhattan Beach Hotel, ca. 1880; publisher unknown. For most New Yorkers, Brooklyn was just a place you went through to get to the beach resorts. Manhattan Beach, which was the eastern quarter of Coney Island, boasted three superb hotels that attracted a wealthy clientele. Of them, the Manhattan Beach was the most impressive. The largest of its kind in the world when it was built in 1877, it was a full 600 feet long, with facilities for serving up to 4,000 meals at a time! Permanent guests stayed on the upper floors, transients below. Easy access was provided to the railroad depot, which was located at the rear of the hotel. The hotel closed in 1910.

147. Iron Steamboat Pier, Coney Island, 1889; Underwood & Underwood. Less affluent visitors to Coney Island could afford only a day trip on a steamboat from the city. There were two great iron steamboat piers for disembarking. The larger, at West Brighton, was 1,000 feet long. Boats left it hourly for the city. The buildings on the pier housed saloons and bathrooms.

148. Pay Department, ca. 1868; E. & H. T. Anthony & Co. Octagonal houses were popular during the first half of the nineteenth century, but it was unusual for an office building such as this one to have been built in that form.

149.   Fire engine, Brooklyn Navy Yard, ca. 1863; publisher unknown. For some inexplicable reason, the publishers of stereographs neglected the subject of New York's fire engines. Consequently, this fine view of a steam pumper at the Navy Yard is especially welcome.

150. Derrick and boilers, Brooklyn Navy Yard, ca. 1875; publisher unknown. This giant wooden derrick was used to hoist sections of a ship and ponderous boilers.

151. North on Main Street, Flushing, ca. 1870; O. C. Smith, Brooklyn. The development of Queens as a suburb of New York was slow. It had a number of small communities, such as Flushing (founded by English settlers in 1642), and some industrial facilities in Long Island City, but overall it was not much different from the rural areas of Suffolk County to the east.